I LOVE LIFE

By Mikias Girma

"Beautiful Always Stays"

Beauty appears and goes
Fading with your spark
Beautiful amazingly glows
Keeping your indelible mark
Beauty gets viewed by the eye
Showing your brief display
Beautiful arrives from the sky
Treasuring your precious array
Beauty frames the fixture
Seeking your timeless art
Beautiful beautifies the picture
Loving from your heart
Beauty strays away
Beautiful always stays

"You Found Beautiful"

Your ideas sound smart
Your voice remains thankful
You give your heart
You search for beautiful
People want to say
Only recall their kindness
Don't let beautiful slip away
You deserve true happiness
Some days wet your eyes
Most nights dream with you
Your spirits belong in the skies
Uplifting thoughts get through
Love makes the heart full
You found beautiful

"I Smile From My Heart"

My heart can't speak
Talking hurts me
My eyes do leak
I walk in the rain sadly
My emotion motions to vent
Holding too much inside
I don't know where the words went
Wanting joy by my side
Joy can't hear
But I listen to my heartbeat
Wonderful things start to appear
I finally feel upbeat
Today shines a new start
I smile from my heart

"The Chapter After"

Your feelings did hurt too much
So you wrote to recover
You discovered a healing touch
Under your heart's cover
Your heartbeat stays upbeat
Turning the page does relax
You and joy meet
Your smiles come back
You found a great story now
Composing a thankful letter
Your heart makes a vow
To keep bliss forever
Happiness writes in your heart
The chapter after you fell apart

"Persistence Finds Brilliance"

You want to excel
Reaching for your stars above
But your sad tears fell
Trying to achieve what you love
Life may give a setback
But you control how you act
Your hope rises back
Positivity keeps the dream intact
You paint your craft diligently
Mind over matter
Trying things differently
To make your art better
Passion goes the extra distance
Persistence finds brilliance

"Silver Lining"

Clouds travel daily
Painting the sky shiny or dark
We may feel happy or empty
But life continues to embark
Sky never looks the same
Moments come and go
Showing reasons why they came
Optimism does glow
For every kind of cloud
We draw a thankful expression
Sunshine comes back around
A brighter side does mention
Every cloud has a silver lining
No matter what, stay smiling

"Heart's Remarkable Mark"

Sunrise seeks an art
You paint with zest
You use your heart
Love draws the best
Your chest does design
Everything that you do
Today requests you to sign
The quest wants to remember you
Your heart gives a signature
Penning your wonderful journey
Your bliss becomes a fixture
Smiling to eternity
Wherever you embark
Leave your heart's remarkable mark

"Stay In Your Lovely Present"

Everyone receives a gift
Every present feels wonderful
Every smile does uplift
Every day shares something meaningful
Your road ahead looks promising
Your heart puts a bow of the sun
Love explores a precious thing
Cherish your only one
Treasured time does rise
Optimism points to a great view
Keep your eyes on the surprise
Appreciate what your life drew
Love today's moment
Stay in your lovely present

"Today Says Celebrate"

Today wants a small party
A great occasion came around
You bring smiley and happy
Positivity gives a musical sound
You continue to invite
Anything with uplifting energy
The air of bliss feels right
Dancing with life's melody
You won't look another way
This moment seems not done
Every day has a song to play
You cherish each one
Tomorrow can wait
Today says celebrate

"Rhythm Of Dreams"

Practice, find and master the rhythm
Of whatever you love to do
Rhythm sings the best system
Dance with your dream come true
Your heart plays uniquely
A song made for you
Memorize the melody
Your dream will ensue
If you hear resistance
Continue to work it
One day with persistence
You'll hear a wonderful hit
Everything has rhythm it seems
Flow with your rhythm of dreams

"My Smiley Way"

I walked away
Trying to find what I lost
I left the rainy way
My heart cried the most
I hope to see sunshine in time
As sadness pushes me downhill
But faith helps me climb
Making my emptiness fill
I arrive at a sign
Joy gives me a gaze
I mimic its wonderful design
Solving my life's maze
Found my sunny day
Around my smiley way

"Happily True"

People's words may hurt
While you paint your art
Faith gifts you comfort
Dream uplifts your heart
Can't control what others do
You don't sway
Your mind controls you
You think of a positive way
You thank your achievement
No matter what it is
You cherish this precious moment
Your self-portrait gives you bliss
No matter what others say or do to you
Feel proud of yourself and stay happily true

"Sky Blue"

When you feel blue
You look up at the lovely sky
Sky blue kindly flew
Drying your heart's cry
Your sad tears disappear
Sky blue mixes a special blend
Its fresh air makes it clear
Its blue stays your best friend
Sky enjoys healing
Painting a happy face
You keep on smiling
Thanking every place
When you feel blue
Sky blue beautifies your view

"My Dream And I Fly"

My heart found a flame
My love does ply
My wish calls one name
My dream will reply
My passion draws on air
Working to accomplish
My faith takes me there
Guiding me to finish
I see my beautiful art
Treasuring this view
It touches my heart
Our love stays true
In this lovely sky
My dream and I fly

"Fortunate Discovers A Fortune"

The main things remain free
Feeling free to love
To help someone's journey
To fly with dreams above
Worth more than money
Brighter than gold
Freedom looks beautifully sunny
Having incredible stories untold
Today gives an opportunity
The price stays priceless
Sky enriches us thankfully
Smiles treasure happiness
Life gifts a special token
Fortunate discovers a fortune

"Remember Your Amazing Worth"

Some things will hurt
Trying to make you feel worthless
But your heart will assert
Having the origin of happiness
Born to shine above
You keep a wonderful mood
Sky's reflection shows love
You mirror feeling good
Even on rainy days
One smile gives shelter
Finding incredible ways
You rise to do better
Precious gave you birth
Remember your amazing worth

"Place Your Gemstone"

The world wants a pure light
We all have one in our hearts
Working day and night
We shine our true arts
Every life works as a team
Putting miracles in the sky
Showing the power of a dream
Luminous stars forever fly
Inspiring others to reach
Each star gives a guide
Always willing to teach
Above smiles so wide
Dreams have shown
Place your gemstone

___

"Your Beautiful Surprise"

Morning makes something special
Giving you a surprise art
Sunrise won't tell
You have to follow your heart
You feel thankful
While going on the journey
Life shows the most incredible
When the heart feels happy
Smiling goes a long way
Dream keeps pace
Love lovely today
Enjoy every place
Open today's skies
Your beautiful surprise

"Pretty Cloud"

Pretty Cloud, what do you carry
A sunny dream or a rainy tear
You seem to show a great story
Covering it as you disappear
Did the dream come true
Or did the cry go away
You always paint sky's view
Beautifying every day
Can you do a delivery
We have a wish for tomorrow
To see a joyful journey
You tell us to follow
To fly, deny worry
Pretty Cloud vowed to carry

"Knock On Wood"

I knock on wood
To stock on good luck
Today answers in a great mood
Pure happiness does unlock
Something also knocks on me
Way deep in my heartbeat
I see my dream waiting patiently
I open my heart to meet
I take it to diligence's door
We finally hear a reply
Love takes me on a tour
Dream lights a fireplace nearby
Life feels good
Knock on wood

"Umbrella"

During life's storm
We might lose power
But sky offers a Dorm
Blessings kindly shower
We might lose light
But we find a candle
Faith gives us sight
Lending a caring handle
We share our bright gift
Helping someone in the rain
Every candle does uplift
Drying eyes to shine again
During life's storm
Caring makes an umbrella form

"One Day Closer"

As your eyes thank morning
Birds sing closer
Your dream wrote you something
Your heart plays the composer
Sky may chorus rain
Or may resonate sunny
Feeling good or pain
You dance to find your one and only
Your heart harmonizes persistence
To travel very long
Believing in every instance
To find your love song
Heart plays life's theme
One day closer to dream

"Your Knowledge Empowers"

Knowledge empowers
Sharing great insight
Studying gives us power
Our minds stay bright
Ideas won't run out
Shining through action
Education maps a wonderful route
Guiding the next generation
Knowledge loves to expand
We all take part
Helping each other understand
Learning by heart
Your mind powers
Your knowledge empowers

"Mind Over Matter"

Regardless of how you feel
Your witty mind controls
Your happy feet move until
You reach your lofty goals
Your body may tire
But your mind doesn't mind
Your heart has a desire
Working hard to find
You won't give in
While giving everything
Your destiny will win
Your destination does sing
You listen to the positive chatter
Mind over matter

"Your Persistence Pays"

Your persistence pays
A visit to your dreams
Your assistance displays
Everywhere faith seems
After you draft your plan
Your goals begin to raft
In your amazing life span
You'll master your craft
You strive in many ways
Giving another try
When your belief stays
Your dreams will fly
You work always
Your persistence pays

"Love Keeps The One"

Ideas come and go away
But one touches your heart
It promises to stay
Dream and you become one part
It takes your breath away
Your idea wants to appear
You continually go its way
Your passion does steer
Your thoughts show it always
Diligence polishes every detail
A dream come true plays
As your heart's curtains unveil
Ideas come and run
Love keeps the one

Mikias Girma

"Beautiful Roots"

Shooting stars light during pursuits
We do this to see how far we came
To also thank our roots
As our dreams carry the flame
We blossom and expand
By loving where we grew from
Our strong roots gave us a hand
Inspiring us to become
We may fall but we always rise
Feeling their presence inside
They see us proudly in the skies
Helping us reach so wide
Giving them thankful tributes
Shootings stars have beautiful roots

"Your Heart Will Say"

Every heart speaks a certain way
Listen to yours
Write its desire today
Create splendid tours
Do not look back
Pages will turn
Dream has a track
Watch bliss return
Take it to a new chapter
Fulfill your heart's quest
To happily ever after
Love will guide you first
Where does love stay
Your heart will say

"The Best Effort"

Every life tells a story
Sounding incredible and unique
Seeking triumph and glory
Writing with heart's ink
Passion speaks to the journey
Diligence says go
Moving towards destiny
Creating an amazing show
The best book reads a goal, heart's theme
The best story scripts how we got through
The best movie shows our dream
The best effort makes dreams come true

"We Make-Believe"

Sometimes we rake
What we thankfully receive
Other times we make
What our imaginations perceive
Our minds can paint anything
We stay limitless
Using positive thinking
We'll find true happiness
Passion pursues the picture
Helping our ideas thrive
Faith puts its mixture
Making our dreams come alive
Until we receive
We make-believe

"The Current"

When trying to find yesterday
We swim against the current
It feels difficult in every way
Making us very spent
We receive help from the stream
It shows tomorrow's reflection
Painting our dream
We change our direction
The waves wave and sing
To encourage our progress
We can do anything
With courage and happiness
We flow with the current
Enjoying the current moment

"The Key"

I opened dream's door
After searching for the key
It had a lock for sure
Good luck smiles at me
I did get stuck
But now I see the light
Faith helps to unlock
By turning wrong to right
Passion finds a way
Persistence will retry
The key does display
Love will pry
Locked dream opens wide
The key stays in the heart inside

"Helpful Bridges"

While our journeys advance
We build a bridge for tomorrow
Giving people the same chance
In case they'd like to follow
Our appreciation will stay
We help them cross
They shine our way
Lighting their smiles across
We don't burn bridges away
We may need assistance, too
Their kindness won't sway
Every bridge's path supports two
The more helpful bridges show
The more places we can all go

"Smiles Overcome"

We can't control rain's pour
But hearts can stay dry
A smile has an umbrella for sure
Covering during the cry
Tears can't touch this place
Positivity finds the brightest way
Designing the face
Making a sunny day
Time heals amazingly
Obstacles seem small
Joy strengthens happily
Standing very tall
Rain may come
Smiles overcome

"Bliss Gave My Heart A Kiss"

I wake up with a smile
My heart met a pretty thing
Everything feels worthwhile
Love makes me sing
I gladly go outside
Loving life truly
I stay by its side
Admiring its beauty
I don't want to say bye
But I have things to do
I ask it to stay nearby
It says I love you
My heart feels bliss
Bliss gave my heart a kiss

"Blank Page Shows A Heart"

I have so much to say
But the paper remains blank
It looks my way
But my feelings sank
My tears pour
My words couldn't float
I hope to endure
Seeing what destiny wrote
I try to copy it
But my hand seems weak
My faith stays lit
Strengthening my heart to speak
Thanking helps me start
Blank page shows a heart

"Positive Thoughts Encourage"

Positive thoughts cheer
When we feel weak
They make wishes appear
Guiding us to the peak
They know the route
Dreams stay there
They tell us all about
Having great ideas to share
Positivity speaks kindly
Supporting us from the start
Helping us see clearly
Shining throughout every art
Dreams give courage
Positive thoughts encourage

"Rock With It"

Life does rock
Moving all around
It finds the best luck
When rolling with heart's sound
Listen to your song inside
It has the soundtrack to joy
Play it on every ride
Dance to completely enjoy
Create your dream show
Your smile lights the stage
Your happy footprints glow
Composing on journey's page
Heart sings a classic hit
Rock with it

"You Have Everything"

You don't have anything
Except your heart
It can also sing
And draw your dream's art
You don't have anything
Except your soul
It stays uplifting
Positive voices console
You don't have anything
Except your smile
Joy does spring
Making each day worthwhile
You don't have anything
You have everything

"Starry Scar"

You have a scar
But you can do anything
It became your lucky star
Gifting you a wing
Some see pain
But you feel a special mark
You and scar will attain
Smiling as you both embark
Scar healed your wound
Its care makes you aware
You both fly around
Making the greatest pair
You reach very far
With your starry scar

"Music To Your Ears"

When negativity speaks your way
Don't spend your time to refute
Ignore and enjoy today
Hearing it go mute
Positivity plays in your ears
Listen to your inner voice
Joy gladly cheers
You made the right choice
Life loves to sing
Using your heartbeat
Happiness has a ring
Keeping you upbeat
When your smile appears
It plays music to your ears

"Sacrifice"

Dream doesn't come easily
It takes hard work
To feel happy
You paint your artwork
Your friends say go out
To have fun
But you decline that route
You found the one
Your love stays
Your goals speak
You put in the time always
You reach the ultimate peak
Dream comes with a price
You receive it with sacrifice

"Be Yourself Always"

Be yourself says sunrise
Rise with this great advice
Learn, listen and memorize
Mesmerize today's skies
Be your amazing name
Not someone's fame
Be your heart's flame
Feel proud of where you came
You will soar
Opening dream's door
Good times treasure and store
Enjoy your life's splendid tour
Put smiling displays
Be yourself always

"Blind Love Finds Lovely"

Love does disappear
Once you meet
Watch happiness appear
In your heartbeat
Heart sees the invisible
Love stays blind
Drawing the most incredible
Truly one of a kind
After you find it
Every place will know
Everything looks lit
Making smiling glow
Touch what you can't see
Blind love finds lovely

"*Forgive And Live*"

You didn't want to forgive
Someone hurt you too much
But your sadness grew to live
Your heart lost touch
The burden felt heavy
Tears filled your broken heart
You couldn't carry
So you looked for a new start
Today helped you find
To pour out your rain
You wanted peace of mind
To see delight again
Forever give
Forgive and live

"Enjoy Your Lifetime"

Your time to relax
To gather your thoughts
To play positive tracks
To minimize doubts
Your time to learn
To improve from yesterday
To cherish every turn
To find the brightest way
Your time to heal
To get stronger
To appreciate the feel
To smile longer
Your heartbeats rhyme
To enjoy your lifetime

"Kindness Stays One Of A Kind"

Nice people don't finish last
Kindness doesn't keep count
A smile moves people fast
Happiness does mount
Giving hearts do race
For a special deed
They place a smiling face
To help someone in need
Feeling good stays
People do care
Contributing in many ways
They'll always be there
Amazing hearts run to find
Kindness stays one of a kind

"Rainbow In Disguise"

Heart may cry all night
Bringing in cold-morning skies
But warm tears stay bright
Pouring a blessing in disguise
Heart will see a reason
Nothing really stays
Sky changes in season
But heart glows always
Showers make it strong
More than yesterday
Sadness doesn't stay long
Happiness colors the way
Every tear in the skies
Lights a rainbow in disguise

"Miracle"

Every heart gives a surprise
For each day since birth
You'll continue to rise
To shine your true worth
Today feels lucky
It appreciates you
Smile on your journey
Your wishes will come true
Many will marvel
As you thankfully achieve
They'll also be able
As you happily perceive
Life stays incredible
You show a miracle

"The Greatest Painter"

I attend an art gallery
To see the greatest painter
It beautifies every journey
Everyone can enter this center
It doesn't cost a dime
Always staying priceless
It'll show you an amazing time
Picture your happiness
You can pose and float above
Today presents a new drawing
It makes dreams and love
Ask it to sketch anything
Sky remains forever
The greatest painter

"Lost And Found"

Broken heart lost someone
It searches with a tear
Clouds cover the sun
Only emptiness comes near
Heart doesn't feel the same
Today asks why
Showers write the name
A wish floats to the sky
Heart wants to glow
In case the missing returns
Love will always show
Memory sees that face as it turns
Two smiles come back around
Lost and found

"Questioning Lights The Quest"

Do ask
What makes you fond
Dreams won't mask
Great ideas respond
Questioning lights the quest
Continue to express
Hear your heart's request
Guiding you to happiness
After listening to your voice
The world will help you
Work on the best choice
To make your dreams come true
To bask
Do ask

"We Stay Fly"

We stay fly
Creating our day
Rainy or shiny sky
We float our dreams' way
We don't look back
Nor do we pause
Our smiles stack
Just for joy, just because
Faith stays in our souls
We spread our wings
Achieving our goals
We can do anything
Dreams light nearby
We stay fly

"Inspiring Words"

Words stay powerful
Needing tender care
They can make life beautiful
Helping any despair
We have a choice
Words allow us to select
Let's hear the positive voice
It has the greatest effect
Some things are better left unsaid
Hurtful words may forgive but won't forget
Some things are better left said
Constructive words live without regret
Memories do cling
Inspiring words mean everything

"My Faith Will Rise"

My eyes can't sleep
My dreams won't show
Should my heart weep
Sky, please let me know
I'll wish on a star
Hoping it sees me
Star doesn't seem too far
Can you hear my plea
Read me a story
Take me to a happy ending
Let me see glory
I trust you with everything
After I close my eyes
My faith will rise

"Make A Vow"

Will you promise
To do one thing
Please don't compromise
It means everything
Yesterday can't change
No matter what you do
Today has great range
Anything can come true
Do what makes you happy
Do think positive
Do paint your destiny
Do smile and stay active
Make a vow
To enjoy now

Mikias Girma

"On Dream's Trail"

You tried your best
But to no avail
Couldn't finish the test
But you didn't fail
Your dream doesn't rest
You rise for the finish-line
Strength comes from your chest
Heartbeats tick a great time
You create your own way
Feeling thankful truly
Getting closer to your day
Running with your destiny
Faith will prevail
On dream's trail

"I Love You"

Sometimes I lose you
But how did I miss
You gave me things to do
You remind me of bliss
You tell me to smile
To cherish the beautiful sky
To make today worthwhile
To keep you nearby
I need you always
You lighten my day
My heartbeat plays
Dancing your way
No matter what I do
Life, I love you

"Forever Feel Enchanted"

Lovely days hug tightly
Lonely nights seem cold
Feel your heart thankfully
Do the great things it told
Life does captivate
Its melody stays indelible
Don't make a minute wait
Do the most incredible
Stand very tall
Fallen will climb
Answer dream's call
Have the greatest time
Appreciate the little things
Take nothing for granted
Life charms everything
Forever feel enchanted

"Smiles Add Ventures"

While you climb life's hill
Fatigue makes you frown
But sky gives you a thrill
After reaching, you look down
Look how far you came
But you have farther to go
You put your dreams in a frame
Allowing joy to show
Your face tells a story
Describing how you feel
To achieve glory
Your steps dance with zeal
To worthwhile adventures
Smiles add ventures

"Dream Does Foreshadow"

Dream leads the way
Destiny shadows its move
They design a wonderful array
Helping you improve
They use your heart's light
Your great insights also lend
They stay with you day and night
Remaining your best friend
They work as an amazing team
You adore what they do
After you have a memorable dream
Your footsteps will make it come true
Destiny follows a shadow
Dream does foreshadow

"Extending Our Journey"

We stated our goal weight
We ate a healthy plate
Great nutrition did create
We await a joyful heart rate
Running also after it
Our diligence didn't sit
Weight scales became lit
Saying we did it; we're fit
Our fitness goals undertook
Making healthy food the best cook
We exercise not only for the mirror look
But also to add chapters in our life book
Healthy feels happy
Extending our journey

"Beautiful Dream Emblems"

They gift us a sign
Amazing things will come
They love to design
Inspiring us to become
They paint in the eyes
From the heart's treasure
Placing it in the skies
Giving pure pleasure
They make a special symbol
To help us see clearly
Attaining won't be simple
But we work diligently
We simply adore them
Beautiful dream emblems

"Smiling Happiness"

Stress doesn't know the address
To your joyful face
You only let in happiness
It has a key to your place
Happiness knits you something
You truly adore
You follow the string
It feels so pure
You'll always wear
No matter where you go
Special moments you'll share
Making each day glow
You do not address any stress
You do knot and dress a smiling happiness

Mikias Girma

"Charm Of Bliss"

Sky looks lovely
But its heart remains half full
Sun wants this beauty
Together, they look beautiful
Sky enjoys to dress
Wearing colors of grace
To feel warm happiness
Sun paces to sky's place
To dance with its love
Sun gives shy sky a chase
Handing roses in a vase above
Sky smiles its luminous face
Sun and sky slowly kiss
Today paints a charm of bliss

"Voiceless Have A Voice"

Voiceless can't speak
But they have so much to say
Their heartbreaks leak
Hoping someone helps their way
If we hear their tears fall
We may be the only few
Let's help them stand tall
Guiding them through
Our voice can lend
Telling their story
The world will be their friend
Assisting their journey
They deserve a choice
Voiceless have a voice

"Calm Drew On Your Palm"

Calm took your hand
Told you to read the art
It helped you stand
Giving you a healthy heart
Your mind found peace
It releases worry
You touch a joyful piece
Calm appeases happily
Your destiny has a map
You hold it always
Tranquility does wrap
You follow its ways
You stay calm
Calm drew on your palm

"Dear Mother"

During my first cry
You hugged me tightly
I saw your beautiful eye
You started my life's journey
During my first day of school
You walked and held my hand
Giving me your heart's tool
Teaching me to proudly stand
During my first church day
You dressed me in my best
You closed my eyes to pray
Putting Faith in my chest
During my first flu
Many got away
So I ran to you
You nursed me all day
During my ups and downs
I can count on my positive force
Your smiles change my frowns
You guide sunshine's course
During my life here
Our bond stays
Thankful to have you near
Dear Mother, I love you always

"Feeling Blessed For Sure"

We can't always get
Everything we seek
But some things we forget
So our blessings speak
They say look at me
We want you to count
So we count and see
Our blessings mount
All the way to the skies
How did we miss
These great things in our eyes
Our hearts now feel bliss
We have so much to be thankful for
Feeling blessed for sure

"Your Talent Presents Moments"

Your talent comes from above
Your effort works day and night
Your passion pursues love
Your hope keeps it bright
Your fall makes it far
Your persistence brings it near
Your heart has a shining star
Your faith does appear
Your positivity thinks of a way
Your patience gets a chance
Your art performs today
Your success begins to dance
Your dream hosts events
Your talent presents moments

"Between Precious Time And Me"

My time won't tell me
My heart ticks inside
Joy stays in my journey
I enjoy my ride
My time keeps a secret
I study to know
Working with my heartbeat
My dream will show
My time stays close
We travel on every endeavor
No matter what I choose
We smile forever together
Between precious time and me
I'll be everything I can be

"Observe"

Whatever we're looking for
May tour very near
But negativity makes it detour
Forcing what we seek to disappear
After clearing the mind
We view tranquility
Positivity will gladly find
Putting wishes in our journey
Dream gives us sight
But love sees the most beautiful
We work for what feels right
Our hearts remain thankful
Thoughtful things serve
Thoughts have to observe

"Yesterday's Curtains Close"

I can't sleep
Sleep doesn't see my eyes
Only sad memories keep
Performing in my cries
My tears can't find dreams
My thoughts paint yesterday
I have tried everything it seems
But sleep won't rest my way
My worries finally go out the door
Pulling down the sad curtain
My eyelids now close to explore
Tranquility lights so certain
My dreams rose
Yesterday's curtains close

"Your Flaw Draws Flawless"

You see many self-reflections
One perspective stays around
Optimism has your attention
Making you feel very proud
Your view tries to be perfect
But imperfection uncovers an art
Joy does reflect
By thanking to start
Time brightens weakness
Feeling stronger by day
A smile does express
Mirroring the shiniest way
Happiness will impress
Your flaw draws flawless

"Always Forever Believe"

When they don't believe
You depend on a few
Your faith won't leave
Your heart also remains true
You can make it
Uplifting things say
Your strong mind stays fit
By positive thinking all day
Your beliefs won't break
You trust your inner voice
It guides you to the peak
Your smiles rejoice
Your heartbeats achieve
Always forever believe

"Thank You Card"

We all have an ace
Shaped of a heart
We show our smiling face
As the games of life start
The card may peal
Feeling the heart break
But time will heal
Every sunrise does remake
We can't control the cards we're dealt
But we can control how we play
No matter how much joy or pain felt
Our appreciation will stay
Giving life the highest regard
We give today a thank you card

"Love To Read And Write"

To learn and succeed
We read and write
Both of them we need
They guide us to the light
Knowledge does feed
Reading gladly inspires
Dreams promise to keep
Writing amazingly transpires
We have so much to say
Painting on paper
Poetic words draw the way
To make us do better
We love to read
We love to write
Writing helps read
Reading helps write

"My Inner Voice And I Rejoice"

I won't be my worst enemy
I'll be my best friend
Delight recites in my journey
Bright words extend
My inner voice speaks loudly
Having the biggest say
It encourages me
Showing me the happiest way
When I feel weak
It makes me strong
Keeping me unique
Singing a beautiful song
I have a choice
My inner voice and I rejoice

"Forgiveness Gives Happiness"

To stay positive
We accept the sorry
Forgive to not relive
We deserve a joyful story
The old chapter feels cold
Tomorrow's pages look promising
Dreams have already told
Our steps write the most amazing
Hurt eases with time
Making us stronger by day
We travel with sunshine
Not looking yesterday's way
Smiles will address
Forgiveness gives happiness

"Better Late Than Never"

I waited for you for so long
Did you get off the wrong stop
Love kept me strong
At night, I looked for you at the top
I feel thankful you came
Please remain by my side
You still look the same
My heart needs your guide
I truly did miss you
Let's catch up today
Following what fate drew
You lead the way
Dream, stay with me forever
Better late than never

"Create To Dedicate"

Create to dedicate
Make someone smile
Your art will relate
It'll be worthwhile
Create amazing bliss
For many to enjoy around
Paint their wish
Using your heart's unique sound
It'll last after you leave
Inspiration floats to endeavor
Help them achieve
Live in their success forever
Smiles will narrate
Create to dedicate

"Picture Your Wonderful Name"

Your name lights above
Blinking your wish
Pursue your love
Feel complete bliss
Your name has a meaning
Meant to do something special
Follow your calling
Make your art sensational
Be proud of where you came
While you reach higher
You rose and overcame
Above picked you to inspire
Stars shine a splendid frame
Picture your wonderful name

Mikias Girma

"You Love What You Do"

Your passion wakes your heart
Your destiny has potential
They tell you to start
To do something special
They open your eyes
Hearing your heart sing
Your goals rise
Saying you can do anything
You truly will
Speaking it into existence
Today climbs uphill
Bridging tomorrow's distance
As dream waits to come true
You love what you do

"Use Heart's Brush"

Art stays in its prime
It doesn't rush
Appreciate your time
Using a special brush
Paint an amazing place
From the soul inside
Destiny will trace
Reach far and wide
Sketch your masterpiece
Resembling dream's view
Today wants a piece
Love the work to do
To feel a rush
Use heart's brush

"Your Goals"

Your goals love to get
Painting your wishes on a note
To help you not forget
Your dreams show what you wrote
Your footprints uniquely trace
Co-signed by your destiny
You mark and keep pace
Following your heart's melody
Some days may tire
But you work thankfully
Your steps reach higher
Moving up gradually
Checkmarks embark to dreams
Your goals script your life's themes

"Patience Shines Essence"

Patience may seem difficult
We want something now
Faith has slowly built
We gradually learn how
As we continue to climb
We cherish the process
Making the best of our time
Finding the true meaning of happiness
Great things wait
Diligence gets closer to the display
Love can create
Enjoying the ride along the way
Each day gives guidance
Patience shines essence

"Enjoy Your Only One"

Life gifts one only
One amazing heart
To cherish many
Appreciate your art
Life presents one sky
With many stars above
Every dream can fly
Pursuing true love
Life draws sunshine
To help many eyes see
Destiny has your design
Achieve in your journey
Today has just begun
Enjoy your only one

"Can't Dim A Gem"

Heart shines a valuable stone
Displaying a genuine design
Even when left alone
It smiles with sunshine
Can't stay broken apart
Broken pieces return
Love stays in the heart
Passion continues to yearn
Might get lost along the way
But heart will find
Even on a dark day
It embarks to one of a kind
Nothing can stem
Can't dim a gem

"You Happily Move On"

Someone did you wrong
But you don't want revenge
You become strong
But your strength won't avenge
You wish the person the best
Focusing on your dream
Your past will rest
Your goals lift you to beam
You won't look back
Your soul stays in the skies
Even if this person does attack
You'll continue to rise
Your good character won
You happily move on

"When Giving A Hand"

When someone needs a hand
Give them two
Help them stand
Even if you have a few
It's the thought that counts
There may come a time
So let our blessings mount
Together we climb
We'll go to a better place
It has space for everyone
Let's build a smiling face
Under the beautiful sun
We all stand
When giving a hand

"I Feel Better"

I don't feel well
Rain surrounds me completely
I try to get out of this spell
My tears spell unhappy
Every drop vents to the floor
Pouring everything I feel
As I try to endure
To make my heart heal
My feelings write
Until my face dries
I see a bright light
Sending my sadness to the skies
My tears go with the letter
I feel better

"Listening Will Amaze"

To become amazing
We try to solve life's maze
Listening tells us everything
Helping our dreams always
Some have been there
Describing the route
They will gladly share
Knowing mostly about
They save us precious time
Teaching us special ways
As we make our climb
Their guidance stays
To solve life's maze
Listening will amaze

"Happy Keeps Me Company"

Misery loves company
So I walked away
Wanting to feel happy
I went sunshine's way
I don't like negativity
Positivity has joy everywhere
Knowing what to say to me
It truly does care
My smile gets found
My mood stays good
My steps have a blissful sound
Knock on wood
Unhappy doesn't work for me
Happy keeps me company

"Be Very Giving"

To give so much
You need to have a lot
Your treasured heart must touch
Caring remains the most sought
Money can't buy joy
It can't see the intangible
The soul offers to enjoy
The spirit feels incredible
Sharing won't run out
Kindness has ample supply
Love brings more about
Delightful smiles light the sky
To have everything
Be very giving

"Drying Silent Tears"

Doesn't say anything
Words get away
Heart walks on a string
Falling on dismay
Heart shatters into many
But no one can hear
Standing and acting happy
Only silent tears come near
Then something uplifts
Making a heart repair
The mood gladly shifts
Above does truly care
Faith always appears
Drying silent tears

"Love Beautifies Beautiful"

Morning does mesmerize
Lifting the dream above
One wish touches the skies
Feelings look for true love
Wanting to care
Heart does long
Having something to share
Dedicating an eternal song
Journey continues to sing
Hoping for a perfect match
One star plays the string
While fate harmonizes a catch
Life feels wonderful
Love beautifies beautiful

"Spark One"

We want to do more
We have plenty
Caring will forever endure
Let's make someone happy
We can heal a heart
To encourage it to fly
Believing in its art
Asking it to brighten the sky
When we help one
This candle will assist many
Kindness lights with the sun
Bliss stays in people's journey
To shine a ton
Let's spark one

"Feel Good Always"

The best mood feels good
You gave your best
You stood and withstood
Passing life's test
Your chest has a treasure
You continue to shine
Pursuing your pleasure
Drawing this precious design
You found your niche
Hearing your calling
You created to enrich
You did something amazing
You gleam in many ways
Feel good always

Mikias Girma

"Respect Does Reflect"

Not only give respect
To the people around
But also keep self-respect
And feel very sound
Respect sounds good
Coming from many voices
It lightens every mood
Giving positive choices
When we respect someone
We respect ourselves
When we respect everyone
We always feel good about ourselves
It has the best effect
Respect does reflect

"Your Thoughts Paint Your Destiny"

Paradise shows a place
For all to visit
Pack your smiling face
Great feelings emit
Imagination loves to draw
Where do you want to go
Look to feel in awe
Focus to make it show
Keep it there
Tomorrow takes a picture
Carry it everywhere
Ideas continue to capture
Positivity lights creativity
Your thoughts paint your destiny

"Run Your Heart's Pace"

With others, you don't race
But your heartbeats run
Carrying a unique case
Looking for the one
Love does lace
Making a special footprint
Your wish moves with grace
Your thanking does sprint
Dream leaves you a trace
As destiny shines near
But you don't chase
Faith will always appear
To see art's place
Run your heart's pace

"Smile For 365 Reasons"

Four seasons share the skies
Painting spectacular days
Life teaches to endure
Searching for meaning always
Your thoughts learn from the past
Your heart dreams of a way
Your great memories last
Some make you feel dismay
Many may like you for many reasons
Some may dislike you for no reason
Whatever the reason
Be like the sun and light every season
During life's seasons
Smile for 365 reasons

"Perfect Your Imperfection"

Everything starts with imperfection
Small details need attention
Big details may be the distraction
But they all need affection
They want your heart's connection
Love truly wants perfection
Pick your best section
Improve it with correction
Don't worry about rejection
Faith gives you protection
Work always with elation
Pass the edit inspection
Stay proud of your art collection
Perfect your imperfection

"I Paint My Broken English"

I had broken English
But I felt smart
Classes and I did finish
I wanted to write art
I did fail as well
Still seeing the red mark
Grammar error and misspell
But my spirit continued to embark
I will know the rules
How did I miss
I study more after finishing school
Trying to find bliss
Today pens a new start
Writing makes me relish
Following my heart
I paint my broken English

"Angels Fly Always"

As my eyes were mourning
For the first time, I saw Angels fly
I kept smiling and crying
Seeing a familiar face in the sky
One Angel asked them to appear
The one who helped raise me
They said you're okay there
You returned to comfort our family
I thought you left forever
But a blessing remembers the ways
Your smile shines forever
In my prayers, your kind soul stays
To you, I dedicate
The rest of my days
To see you again, I can't wait
Angels fly always

"The Beauty Of A Classy Lady"

You look very classy
You learn well in class
You dress your inner beauty
You respect yourself and pass
History class says it's a man's world
But you rewrite it elegantly
Every human has a right since birth
With the stars, you rise gracefully
Your mind stays your strongest muscle
Your creative thoughts light bliss
You work hard and hustle
You simply inspire, Miss
You allow wonderful things to come close
You make yourself and family happy
The sky gives you a pretty rose
The beauty of a classy lady

"You Always Help Me"

When you make me cry
You help me
When you deny my dream's try
You motivate me
When you say no
You push me
When you say I don't know
You educate me
Whatever you do
You improve me
When you stay true
You inspire me
When you assist
You move me
When I help and insist
You humble me
I control my destiny
You always help me

"Paint Your Heart's Art"

Your heart carries an art
We're all wonderful artists
From yours, don't depart
Sketch what it consists
Give it your voice inside
Speak forever long
Your dream reaches so wide
Sing your internal song
It may make us smile or cry
Bringing back a fond memory
Your life touches the sky
Share your incredible story
Today says start
Paint your heart's art

Mikias Girma

"Redemption"

My heart feels redemption
My art sings a theme
My mistakes hug affection
My takes pursue a dream
My talk stays positive
My walk helps me stand
My fate will happily give
My faith takes its hand
My mishaps stay behind
My bliss claps with me
My smile laps on my mind
My love wraps my journey
Above glows liberation
Love shows redemption

BLESSED

Blessings
Light
Everywhere
So
Smile
Every
Day